Writers Who Changed the World

ANNE FRANK

Anita Croy

LUCENT PRESS

Published in 2020 by
Lucent Press, an Imprint of Greenhaven Publishing, LLC
353 3rd Avenue
Suite 255
New York, NY 10010

Produced for Lucent by Calcium
Editors: Sarah Eason and Tim Cooke
Designers: Paul Myerscough and Lynne Lennon
Picture researcher: Rachel Blount

Picture credits: Cover: Shutterstock: Borsvelka; Inside: Shutterstock: Africa Studio: p. 39t; Akturer: p. 40; Anton_Ivanov: pp. 7b, 39c; Tony Baggett: p. 50; Edwin Butter: p. 57; Catwalker: p. 61b; Hans Engbers: p. 48; Everett Historical: pp. 16, 18, 27, 34; Ronald Wilfred Jansen: pp. 8, 11, 30b, 38, 52, 56; Kavalenkava: p. 58; Lario: p. 36; Pablopicasso: p. 37; Posztos: p. 19; Yakovlev Sergey: p. 31; Takashi Images: p. 42; Vyntage Visuals: p. 35; Markus Wissmann: p. 61t; Wikimedia Commons: Bilsen, Joop van/Anefo: p. 45; Blueduck4711: p. 54; Rob Bogaerts/Anefo: p. 29; Bungle: p. 22; Heather Cowper: p. 46; Jac. de Nijs/Anefo: p. 47; Jack de Nijs/Anefo: pp. 51t, 59; Diliff: p. 26; Fotocollectie Rijksvoorlichtingsdienst, Fotograaf Onbekend: pp. 9, 21b; Anne Frank: p. 51b; Immanuel Giel: p. 32; Gonzalort1: p. 49; Ernst Hofmann or Bernhard Walte: p. 25; Eric Koch/Anefo: p. 55; Christian Michelides: p. 60; Pahl, Georg: p. 17; Rossem, Wim van/Anefo: pp. 24, 28; Lt. Arnold E. Samuelson: p. 41t; SS: p. 21t; Unknown: pp. 4, 7t, 10, 12, 15t, 15b, 20, 30t, 41b.

Cataloging-in-Publication Data

Names: Croy, Anita.
Title: Anne Frank / Anita Croy.
Description: New York : Lucent Press, 2020. | Series: Writers who changed the world | Includes glossary and index.
Identifiers: ISBN 9781534565784 (pbk.) | ISBN 9781534565791 (library bound) | ISBN 9781534565807 (ebook)
Subjects: LCSH: Frank, Anne, 1929-1945--Juvenile literature. | Jewish children in the Holocaust--Netherlands--Amsterdam--Biography--Juvenile literature. | Jews--Netherlands--Amsterdam--Biography--Juvenile literature. | Amsterdam (Netherlands)--Biography--Juvenile literature.
Classification: LCC DS135.N6 C79 2020 | DDC 940.53'18092 B--dc23

Printed in the United States of America

CPSIA compliance information: Batch #BS19KL: For further information contact Greenhaven Publishing LLC, New York, New York at 1-844-317-7404.

Please visit our website, www.greenhavenpublishing.com. For a free color catalog of all our high-quality books, call toll free 1-844-317-7404 or fax 1-844-317-7405.

CONTENTS

CHAPTER 1

This photograph of Anne studying was taken in 1940.

ANNE FRANK
Biography

Born: June 12, 1929

Place of birth: Frankfurt, Germany

Mother: Edith Holländer Frank

Father: Otto Heinrich Frank

Famous for: Writing a diary while she and her family were hiding from the Nazis in a secret annex, or apartment, in Amsterdam in the Netherlands.

How she changed the world: Anne's diary showed the world the horrific effect of the Nazi persecution of the Jews on an ordinary teenager and her family. It became a strong symbol for world peace.

Anne Frank's diary SHOWED the world what it was LIKE to SUFFER firsthand the CRUELTY of PERSECUTION. It gave a VOICE to the JEWISH experience of the HOLOCAUST and the TERROR of living under NAZI occupation.

Anne Frank

DRIVEN FROM GERMANY

Annelies Marie Frank was born on June 12, 1929, in Frankfurt, Germany. Although she was named Annelies, her family always called her Anne. Anne had one sister, Margot, who was three years older. The Frank family was wealthy. Otto, her father, was a successful businessman and Anne's mother, Edith, was a housewife. Otto had served in the German army in World War I (1914–1918).

Anne's early childhood was happy, but problems were growing for Jewish Germans like the Franks. After the country's defeat in World War I, Germany had been plunged into economic and social chaos. A politician named Adolf Hitler claimed he could make Germany a great country again. He gradually gained more support for his Nazi Party, which was modeled on military-style discipline. Hitler encouraged his followers to hate Jewish people. The Nazis blamed the Jews for all of Germany's problems.

... problems were growing for Jewish Germans like the Franks.

In 1933, when Anne was four years old, Hitler used the Nazis' success in national elections to have himself made chancellor, or leader, of Germany. Otto could see that life for Jews in Germany would become difficult, so he moved his family to Switzerland. There, they lived with one of Anne's grandmothers. But Otto feared that Switzerland was not safe, either. He decided to move to Holland (now called the Netherlands) from where he hoped to emigrate to Great Britain or the United States.

Words that changed the world

On Saturday, June 20, 1942, Anne wrote in her diary that it feels strange for her to write down her thoughts, because she has never written before. She says that she is just an ordinary teenage schoolgirl and that her writings will be of no interest to anyone. But she loves writing, and it helps her get things off her chest.

Adolf Hitler addressed the German parliament after becoming the country's leader in 1933.

Exploring the text

When Anne started her diary, she had no idea what would happen to her or what kinds of things she would end up writing about. She was a typical teenager who felt a strong urge to share all her feelings but had no one to share them with. The diary became her confidant. Anne told her diary just how she felt about her parents and her sister. She confided in her diary about crushes she had on boys and boys who she thought liked her. She wrote about what she wanted to do when she got older, and about how hard it was to be a teenager. Anne's world could be that of any teenager today—except she and her family were Jews living during the Nazi persecution of Jews in World War II (1939–1945).

This recreation from a museum shows Anne writing in her diary.

LIFE IN HOLLAND

After Anne and her family arrived in Amsterdam in February 1934, life continued as it had been in Germany. Otto had moved to Amsterdam because he spoke Dutch. Many Dutch people wanted to help German Jews, so the Franks were welcomed. The family moved to a new apartment and Otto started a new business. Margot and Anne went to a Montessori school, where they soon learned to speak Dutch fluently. They had a lot of friends to play with. Many of their friends were other German Jews who had come to Amsterdam with their families. The sisters skated on the city's canals in the winter when the water froze and one summer they went to the beach and swam in the sea. At school, Anne was known to be a chatterbox who loved history, reading and writing, and learning about Greek myths. She hated math!

The classroom where Anne and Margot studied at the Montessori school is still used for teaching today.

Under occupation

Life changed on May 10, 1940. World War II had begun in September 1939. Now, German aircraft bombed Amsterdam and the port of Rotterdam, killing thousands of people. Five days later, the Dutch surrendered and German soldiers occupied Holland. Soon the Nazis' swastika flag was flying from buildings across Amsterdam. A few Jewish families escaped from Holland, but it was too late for the Frank family. Anne's grandmother was too sick to move, so they were stuck.

German soldiers rounded up Dutch citizens they suspected of being Jews after their occupation of Holland.

New laws

The Germans introduced laws to limit the freedom of Jewish people. At the time, Amsterdam was home to about 75,000 Jews. All Jews had to register with the Nazis. Jews were no longer allowed to own businesses, so Otto Frank had to give his business to his non-Jewish business partners. Jewish children had to attend special schools, so Anne and Margot had to leave their Montessori school and their friends.

HISTORY'S STORY

Under the anti-Jewish laws, Dutch Jews had to wear a yellow star on their clothes to identify themselves. They were forbidden to use trams, cars, and bicycles, so they had to walk everywhere. They could only shop in Jewish-run stores. They had to stay home between 8:00 p.m. and 6:00 a.m. They could not go to the movies or the theater. They could not even visit Christian friends in their homes.

INTO HIDING

The Franks lived under the strict German laws for two years. During that time, daily life for Jews in Holland became more and more restricted. Otto Frank could see that things were only going to get worse. Stories began to appear from eastern Europe of concentration camps where the Nazis sent Jews and other groups they did not like to carry out forced labor. Otto applied to move his family to England, but his application was rejected.

The territories Germany occupied during the war were governed by military leaders under military laws.

Otto could only see one solution. He would take his family into hiding and wait for the war to end. Only the defeat of Germany would allow life to return to normal. Since spring 1942, Otto and Edith had been secretly planning to move into a hidden annex above a warehouse behind Otto's office. Over several months, they moved furniture to the annex, including a stove and a toilet, and stores of dried food. Once they had prepared everything they would need for a long stay, they would tell the girls and move in. They planned to move on July 16, 1942.

A change of plan

The move was suddenly brought forward. On Sunday, July 5, 1942, Margot received a letter. She was now 16 years old. The letter was an official summons telling her that she was now required to serve in a labor camp in Germany. The Franks knew that a labor camp was another name for a concentration camp, where Jews were kept in prisonlike conditions. Like other Dutch Jews, the Franks had heard that nobody came out of the concentration camps alive. Otto and Edith decided that they could no longer wait to go into hiding. If they did, Margot would be sent away.

The next day, Monday, July 6, Otto and Edith woke their daughters at 5:30 a.m. and told them to get dressed. Not wanting to call attention to themselves by carrying suitcases, the family put on as many clothes as they could. Anne put on two shirts, three pairs of pants, a dress, a skirt, a jacket, a raincoat, two pairs of stockings, heavy shoes, a cap, and a scarf. Then the family left their home and walked toward Otto's office in the rain to begin their new life.

This is the bookstore where Otto bought his daughter a diary as a birthday present. It is still open.

HISTORY'S STORY

The month before the family went into hiding, Anne celebrated her 13th birthday on June 12. Her father gave her a diary with a red checked cover and a padlock. On the inside cover of her new diary, Anne stuck a photograph of herself. She wrote her first entry on June 14. The last entry was written on August 1, 1944, three days before she was discovered.

CHAPTER 2

Adolf Hitler gives the Nazi salute during a parade.

NAZI EUROPE
Background

Anti-Semitism definition: Hatred of and hostility toward Jews

First anti-Jewish laws introduced in Germany: 1933

Status of Jews under the Nazis: Not German citizens, no right to vote

Kristallnacht: November 9–10, 1938. Nazis burned 250 synagogues, and 7,000 Jewish business were looted.

Final Solution: 1941–1945. Planned extermination of all Jews in Nazi-occupied Europe

Death toll: It is estimated that 6 million European Jews were killed by the Nazis. This mass murder is known as the Holocaust.

Anne's diary gives us a WINDOW into the world of NAZI occupation. Her WORDS reveal the TERROR she and her family EXPERIENCED while hiding in the annex. We read about Anne's HOPES for the future, but also her DESPAIR, and we feel the FEAR of a person who lives under the daily THREAT of discovery.

RISE OF THE NAZIS

In 1918, Germany surrendered at the end of World War I. The victorious Allies—the United States, Great Britain, and France—forced Germany to pay huge fines that left the country almost bankrupt. As unemployment rose and life got harder, one man began to promise Germans that he could make things better. Adolf Hitler became a politician in 1918, when he joined a small workers' political party. Hitler quickly rose to lead the party, and in 1920 he renamed it the National Socialist German Workers Party, known as the Nazis. By 1933, the Nazis did so well in German elections that Hitler was able to become the chancellor of Germany. To his followers, he was known as the Führer, or leader.

... one man began to promise ... that he could make things better.

Hitler blamed the Jews for all of Germany's problems, and many Germans agreed with him. Many of the most successful businesses in Germany were owned and run by Jews. When the Nazis started to persecute German Jews by stripping them of their citizenship and taking away their civil rights, many Germans went along with them. Nazi rule was based on fear and violence. People who disagreed with the Nazis or defended the Jews could be imprisoned or even put to death. Hitler remained in charge of Germany until his suicide in April 1945, when it was clear that the war was lost.

Words that changed the world

In 1943, Anne writes that things are getting worse for the Jews. Day and night people are dragged from their homes, and allowed to take just a few possessions with them. And then these possessions are stolen on the journeys the Jews make to the concentration camps. She writes that families are separated and mothers are taken from their children. Children even return from school to find that their parents have been taken away.

Exploring the text

In her diary, Anne describes the reality of life for Jews in Holland and the other countries that the Nazis had occupied. Jews were rounded up and taken away. No one really knew what awaited the Jews who were removed, but Anne's words show that rumors had even reached the secret annex. By 1943, there were many stories about the concentration camps in Germany and Poland. Friends and relatives sent to the camps never returned. The true horror of the concentration camps and death camps did not become completely clear, however, until close to the end of the war.

This photograph shows a Nazi guard standing outside a Jewish store with a sign telling Germans not to shop there.

Jews in Warsaw, Poland, were rounded up and sent to the concentration camps.

PERSECUTING THE JEWS

The Nazis blamed Jews for all the problems Germany suffered after the end of World War I in 1918. As his popularity grew, Hitler gave many speeches to his supporters in which he told them that Jews were an inferior race. Every year from 1923 to 1938, Hitler addressed huge crowds at large gatherings called rallies in Nuremberg in southern Germany. The city was the headquarters of the Nazi Party. On these occasions, Hitler worked the admiring Nazis into a frenzy by insisting that something had to be done to solve what he called "the Jewish problem." He said the only answer to Germany's problems was to get rid of its Jews.

Nazi posters depicted Jews as an evil presence in Germany.

Hitler was supported in his ideas by his closest generals. One of those, Heinrich Himmler, came up with an idea the Nazis called the "Final Solution to the Jewish problem." When the Nazis came to power in 1933, they began to build large camps to imprison both their political enemies and large numbers of Jews. Between 1933 and 1945, the Nazis and their allies would build more than 40,000 prison camps across Europe. They became known as concentration camps, because they "concentrated" the Nazis' victims in one place.

The Final Solution

Himmler's "Final Solution" was the extermination of Europe's Jews by mass murder. The Nazis transported hundreds of thousands of Jews from occupied territory to death camps, such as Auschwitz in Poland. There, Jews were killed with poison gas in special gas chambers that were built to look like large shower rooms. The Jews were told they were to take a shower and pushed into the chamber, and then the gas was switched on.

Nazis burn books in Berlin, Germany.

A certain fate

Other groups the Nazis disapproved of were also sent to the camps. They included Roma people, homosexuals, and the disabled. When the Franks' hiding place was discovered, they knew what fate awaited them, because stories about the camps had spread in Europe. At the peak of the Holocaust, 6,000 people were gassed to death every day at just two camps, Auschwitz and Bergen-Belsen. Historians believe more than 3 million people were murdered in the camps.

HISTORY'S STORY

In May 1933, Nazi students gathered in a square outside the National Opera House in Berlin. They burned about 25,000 books by Jewish writers and other authors the Nazi Party judged to be "undesirable." The book burning was a clear sign of the Nazis' intolerance of any ideas they did not like.

OCCUPIED EUROPE

The Nazis presented German workers as heroic figures.

During the 1930s, the Nazi Party began the persecution of Jews in Germany. It also promoted the idea that true Germans were part of a superior race. According to the Nazis, the Aryans were the ancient Germanic race. They often had blue eyes and blond hair, like many modern Germans. Adolf Hitler wanted to rid Europe of non-Aryan peoples, such as the Jews and the Slavs who lived in eastern Europe. He started to invade Germany's neighbors. He said he was reclaiming German territory to create "living room" for the Aryans. On September 1, 1939, the Nazis invaded Poland. The invasion started World War II, which would last until 1945.

Early in the war, Germany invaded five European countries. Some were invaded for strategic and economic reasons. Others, including Belgium, Holland, and France, were invaded and then occupied. Their citizens lived under Nazi rule and had to follow harsh Nazi laws. Anyone caught disobeying the laws or resisting Nazi rule could be put to death or sent to one of more than 40,000 detention camps.

Enemies of the Nazis

At first, the Nazis imprisoned anyone they saw as inferior or who did not agree with them. It was only later that they started to use some of the concentration camps to carry out large numbers of killings. Six months after Heinrich Himmler introduced the "Final Solution," the first mass gassing took place in December 1941 at Chelmno, Poland. Nazi soldiers gassed Jews and Roma people in special mobile gas vans. The Nazis then started to build larger permanent facilities such as Auschwitz to kill even more people more efficiently. The new camps had gas chambers and ovens for burning bodies.

Jews and other victims arrived at Auschwitz by train along this railroad.

HISTORY'S STORY

In 1933, when the Franks left Germany, there were more than 500,000 German Jews. In the next six years, more than half of them fled. Otto chose Holland because the Dutch people were opposed to Nazi policies. He tried to relocate to the United States in 1938 and 1941, but his application was turned down and the family stayed put.

TIMELINE OF THE NAZI OCCUPATION OF HOLLAND

1940 **May 10:** Nazis attack Holland.

May 13: Dutch government flees to London with Queen Wilhelmina. (They remain in exile for five years.)

May 14: Center of Rotterdam destroyed by bombing.

May 15: The Dutch surrender to the Nazis. Holland is now an occupied country.

Anti-Jewish Decrees in Holland

1940 **October:** Every government official must declare that there is no Jewish blood in his immediate family.

December: People of German blood banned from working for Jewish families.

German bombing left the port of Rotterdam reduced to ruins.

This poster urges Dutch recruits to join the Schutzstaffel, or SS, an elite Nazi paramilitary organization.

1941 **January 10:** All Jewish citizens forced to register. They are given identity cards marked with a "J."

February 22–23: Jews are arrested in Amsterdam.

March: The Nazis begin to confiscate Jewish property.

August: Jewish children can only attend Jewish schools.

November: All Jewish officials and public servants are forced to register with the Germans. More than 2,500 Jewish officials lose their positions.

1942 **January:** Forced labor camps for Jews established in Holland.

May: Jews must wear a yellow star with "Jew" written on it on their outer clothes.

July: The first Dutch Jews are deported to extermination camps in Poland.

1943 **May 1:** Announcement that all remaining Jews are to be removed from Holland.

Soldiers force Dutch Jews to clean the street on their knees.

CHAPTER 3

The bookcase that hid the annex

THE DIARY OF A YOUNG GIRL

Masterwork

Key facts about Anne's Diary:

Diary written: June 14, 1942–August 1, 1944

Language of diary: Dutch

Form of diary: A series of letters addressed to "Kitty"

Number of versions of the diary: Two

Version One: In the red checked diary and two other notebooks

Version Two: Written on loose paper in 1944 after a radio appeal asked Dutch people to keep diaries of their experiences during the occupation.

Anne's DIARY was a SOURCE of COMFORT to her. It allowed her to EXPRESS her THOUGHTS and FEELINGS during what must have been an incredibly TRAUMATIC time for the teenager.

INSPIRATIONS

Anne's diary records just how small the secret annex was. It occupied two floors, but the whole space only covered 50 square yards (42 sq m). It was hidden behind a bookcase in Otto Frank's office building. A secret door led to two rooms. The first was used as a kitchen during the day and a bedroom at night. The other was a bedroom. There was also a small bathroom. On the floor above were two more bedrooms.

A steep staircase led to the two bedrooms at the top of the building.

Anne's diary records just how small the secret annex was.

In this tiny space lived not only the four members of the Frank family—Anne, Margot, Otto, and Edith—but also three members of another family. This was the van Pels family, Hermann, Auguste, and their son Peter. Hermann van Pels was a business colleague of Otto Frank. About four months later, a dentist named Fritz Pfeffer also moved into the annex. Anne wrote that she was not very pleased about his arrival. She had to share a room with Pfeffer and she soon discovered that he snored. In the diary, Anne gave the van Pels and Pfeffer false names. This may have been to disguise them if the book was ever found.

Words that changed the world

In September 1942, Anne writes that her diary has been a huge source of comfort to her, as has "Kitty," to whom she regularly writes. Anne lives for the moments when she can write to Kitty, and confide her deepest thoughts and feelings.

Exploring the text

Early in her diary, Anne complains that she does not really have anyone to whom she can tell her truest feelings, even though she has her family and a lot of friends. She was not very close to her sister, Margot. Anne starts her diary as a way of recording her feelings as a 13-year-old girl. Soon, she decides that what she really wants is for her diary to be like a friend, whom she names Kitty. From then on (June 20, 1942), Anne tells Kitty everything. Once the family goes into in hiding, writing in her diary also helps Anne overcome her boredom.

These Hungarian Jews are waiting to board trains that will take them to concentration camps in Poland.

HISTORY'S STORY

Anne's diary does not just focus on life in the annex. She also describes bombing raids and the course of the war. She refers to the terrible things the Nazis are doing to Jews. She describes the risks the family's friends take to bring them fresh food and news. When she talks about the Franks' boring food and worn-out clothes, we see a little of how difficult it was to be in hiding.

WRITING THE DIARY

Anne was just like any teenager. She covered the walls of her bedroom in the annex with pictures of movie stars cut out of magazines. Anne also loved royal families and wrote about them in her diary. She was particularly interested in the British royal princesses, Elizabeth (now Queen Elizabeth II) and Margaret. She first dreamed of being a movie star, but then decided that what she really wanted to do when she grew up was to write. She saw keeping a diary as a great way of practicing for her future career.

In the diary, Anne often recounts fighting with her mom. She believed that her mom preferred her sister, Margot. Even in hiding, the Franks resembled many other families. Anne recorded arguments about who did the chores and who got in trouble more often. She believed Margot had an easier life than she did. She repeatedly mentions that she feels Margot is treated better because her sister is better behaved.

Anne was fascinated by stories of the British royal family, who stayed at Buckingham Palace in London throughout the war.

Anne writes about how much she loves her father and how much she admires him. In contrast, she does not like Hermann van Pels. She spends a lot of time in her diary criticizing his behavior.

A U.S.bombing raid over Europe

Being a teenager

Just like most teenage girls, Anne thinks about having a boyfriend. She develops a crush on Peter van Pels, who is a few years older than her, and spends much time in her diary discussing him. One day, they even share a kiss. She writes about how the other residents of the annex think she is spoiled, but she defends herself strongly. She is very funny in her descriptions of Fritz Pfeffer and what it is like to share a room with a man who snores every night. She is also very honest. She describes, for instance, how hard it is to go to the bathroom when everyone can hear you.

The diary also explains just how scared Anne was a lot of the time. She hated nighttime bombing raids, even though she knew the Allies were trying to help her. Anne would run to her father at night to protect her. She poured out her fears and hopes every day. The nights were very hard, and she longed for the day when she could go outside once more to feel the sun on her face and smell the grass.

The diary was not just a place to record the daily life of the annex. Anne wrote about her childhood, she made up stories, and she talked about the war. The members of the annex listened to the news on the radio, so they knew how the war was going. Every time the Allies gained a victory, it raised their hopes.

ACTION BREAKDOWN

Anne and her family were in hiding for more than 650 days. For long parts of that time, not very much happened and there was little they could do to keep themselves entertained. Anne became very bored, although she never forgot that it was better to be bored than to be discovered. On more than one occasion, the warehouse below their quarters was broken into by thieves and the residents of the annex had a very anxious wait to make sure that their hiding place had not been discovered.

These are the windows of the living room and the upstairs bedroom of the annex.

A close escape

The worst occasion was on Tuesday, April 11, 1944. When the warehouse was robbed, police came to investigate. They got as far as the office with the bookcase in front of the secret door. One of the residents had left a light on that gave away the existence of the hidden annex, but luckily the policemen did not notice anything unusual. Everyone hiding upstairs was terrified. From then on, they changed their behavior to make sure they made less noise. They no longer opened their windows at night or put the lights on after dark.

Difficult conditions

Normal days in the annex were broken up by visits from Miep Gies, Otto's former secretary, and other office workers. These volunteers brought food and other supplies, and gossip from the outside world. The families also got news from newspapers and the radio. The more time they spent together, however, the more the Franks and the van Pels quarreled. Anne repeatedly tells her diary that it is only her father who is able to rise above the daily squabbles.

After Miep Gies got married, her husband Jan joined the effort to look after the people in the annex.

At night, when the warehouse was empty, everyone would go downstairs to the empty offices. Anne liked to peek out of the window and watch the people in the streets. Winter was the worst time because it got dark so early. By 4:30 p.m., the annex was dark but they could not turn any lights on in case they were spotted. With nothing to do, they even tried to exercise in the dark.

HISTORY'S STORY

Some of the brightest points in Anne's diary are the visits by Miep Gies. Miep was very brave. Most mornings before the other workers arrived, Miep collected a shopping list. She or one of the other helpers—Bep, Victor, and Johannes—returned at lunchtime with food, newspapers, and books. She was their link to the outside world.

KEY CHARACTERS

Anne Frank

The Franks

Anne Frank: (writer) Died of typhus in Bergen-Belsen concentration camp, late February/early March 1945.

Otto Frank: (father) Survived and returned to Amsterdam. Lived until 1980.

Anne Frank memorial

Edith Frank: (mother) Died of exhaustion in Auschwitz concentration camp, January 1945.

Margot Frank: (sister) Died of typhus in Bergen-Belsen concentration camp, February 1945.

Other Residents of the Annex

Hermann van Pels: (Otto's business partner) Gassed in Auschwitz, September 1944.

The cemetery at Bergen-Belsen

Auguste van Pels: (wife of Hermann) Died somewhere in either Germany or Czechoslovakia between April 9–May 8, 1945.

Peter van Pels: (son of Hermann) Died of exhaustion at Mauthausen concentration camp, May 10, 1945.

Fritz Pfeffer: (dentist of Auguste) Died in sick bay of Neuengamme concentration camp on December 20, 1944.

Helpers

Miep Gies: Survived the war. Died in Hoorn, Netherlands, in 2010, aged 100.

Victor Kugler: Imprisoned by the Nazis, but escaped on March 28, 1945. Emigrated to Canada in 1955. Died in Toronto in 1981.

Johannes Kleiman: Imprisoned and released due to ill health on September 18, 1944. Died in Amsterdam in 1959.

Elisabeth Voskuijl: Survived the war. Died in Amsterdam in 1983.

CHAPTER 4

A mural of Anne at a German school

DARK WORLD
Key Themes

Key themes of the diary:

- Being a teenager
- Family
- Loss
- Hope
- Religion
- Friendship
- Sacrifice
- Isolation
- Mortality
- Identity
- Love
- Selfishness

Anne writes that she HOPES she will not have LIVED in vain. She wants to be USEFUL and to even go on LIVING after her DEATH, thanks to her diary. Anne could not have REALIZED at the time of WRITING how POWERFUL her words were.

GROWING UP

One of the main themes of Anne's diary is growing up. The fact that Anne is stuck in the annex does not make it any less difficult for her than for other teenagers as their relationships with other people develop. Being stuck in close confinement with both her own family and the van Pels makes Anne's feelings very intense.

One of the main themes of Anne's diary is growing up.

Anne does not think anyone understands her, with the possible exception of Peter. She describes her sister Margot as studious, quiet, and obedient. This frustrates Anne, who is much more lively and outspoken. Anne is also a modern girl for her time. She discusses the changes in her body, for example, and her feelings for boys. When she describes to Peter the difference between boys and girls, by contrast, he is very shocked.

This poster shows an American teenager during the war. At the same time, Anne was cooped up in the annex.

Words that changed the world

In 1944, Anne writes that her family do not notice her innermost feelings, and she is grateful for that. She says that each day she grows colder and more scornful of her mother, and less caring toward her father. She does not want to share anything with her sister, Margot. Anne says she has closed up "tighter than a drum."

Exploring the text

From Anne's diary entry, the turmoil of being a teenager is clear to see. Anne finds being cooped up with her family very difficult. She feels that even her beloved father no longer really understands her. Her long-running irritation with her mother is something that she shares with millions of other teenage girls. When she needs to be alone, Anne goes up to the attic, taking her diary with her. She increasingly feels that her imaginary friend Kitty is the only person who knows and understands the real Anne. She goes on to say that she is worried that her personality is too lively for her ever to become Peter's girlfriend.

German teenage girls were encouraged to regularly exercise. In contrast, Anne was stuck in a tiny space with little opportunity to move around.

HISTORY'S STORY

Being a teenage girl in the cramped annex was very difficult. There was no privacy. Anne documented all the strangeness and confusion she felt as she went through puberty.

LOSS

For Anne, the cat she had to abandon became a symbol of everything the family had lost.

At the heart of the diary are the themes of loss, isolation, and mortality, which is the inevitability that everyone will die. From the first entry in the diary, when Anne is free but living in an occupied country, the reader is aware of all the things the Franks, like other Jews, have had taken away by the new government. The Franks have lost not just most of their material possessions but also their status in society. Anne does not like this feeling of deprivation, but she is mature enough to understand that, while they are still alive, the family should count themselves lucky.

A beloved pet

One of the things Anne misses most in the annex is her cat, Moortje. The family got Moortje in early 1942, but when they went into hiding, they left the cat with a family friend. Anne misses her every day and cannot bear it when people talk about her to pass the time. She loves her cat so much that she often dreams about her. Peter brings his cat Mouschi into the annex and there is also a warehouse cat, named Moffie, to catch the rats that live in the building. Anne enjoys having these cats around—but they are not the same as Moortje.

An isolated life

Living in the annex isolates Anne in many ways. As well as experiencing a loss of physical freedom, she is trapped among a group of people she often feels do not want to understand her. The pressures of puberty and hiding mean that she has to draw on all her emotional strength to make the best of a terrible situation. Often she feels unable to do that, which makes her feel both angry and sad.

These are empty bags and suitcases taken from Jews on arrival in a concentration camp.

HOPE

Otto's radio was one of the family's most important links to the outside world.

Given her situation and the threats she faces with her family, Anne is remarkably positive and hopeful most of the time. Being in hiding makes her think about the simple pleasures of life, such as feeling the sun on her face and talking to her friends. If she ever leaves the annex, she writes, she knows that she will appreciate these simple experiences much more.

Anne hopes that one day she will be free. She records every Allied advance in the war. She and her father listen to the radio and read smuggled newspapers. They realize that the Nazis are slowly losing control of Europe. Anne looks forward to the future, dreaming of being a writer whose work makes a difference to people's lives.

An inspirational friend

Apart from Kitty, Anne's greatest friend is Miep. She wants to be more like Miep, whose loyalty and friendship are a highlight of her life in hiding. The risks that Miep and the others take for the family make Anne feel humble. Their willingness to potentially sacrifice their lives to help others is perhaps the greatest example of bravery and hope in the diary. Miep's friendship is also an inspiration. Before going into hiding, Anne valued her friends highly. One of the most painful aspects of being in the annex was losing them.

The family observed Jewish rituals in the annex, including lighting the menorah to celebrate Hanukkah.

Comfort from faith

Anne's Jewish religion gives her hope, but it is also what has condemned her family to take shelter in the annex. The family are punished because they are Jews, but being Jewish is still of great comfort to Anne. She gains strength from the centuries of history during which the Jews have successfully managed to overcome persecution. This helps her understand the position in which she and her family find themselves. Studying the past and her position in history helps Anne accept what is happening to her.

This waxwork of Anne writing her diary comes from a museum in Amsterdam.

HISTORY'S STORY

Like any teenager, Anne has dreams and hopes. What makes the diary so touching is that we know what happens to Anne before we even start reading. When she talks about her future, we know that it will never happen. We know that her dreams will not come true. When she fears being discovered, we know that the family will be found and that Anne's story will end in early death.

HOLOCAUST STATISTICS

Number of Jews in Europe before 1933:
Approximately 6.5 million (60 percent of world total)

Total number of Jews murdered in Holocaust:
An estimated 6 million

A sign from Auschwitz saying "Work makes you free"

Number of Jews in Europe in 1950:
3.5 million (2 million in the Soviet Union)

Number of Jewish children killed:
1.1 million

Number of homosexuals killed:
Between 3,000 and 5,000

Number of mentally ill killed:
200,000

Liberated survivors of a concentration camp

Number of Roma killed:
Between 220,000 and 500,000

Number of Nazi extermination camps:
Six, all in occupied Poland

Total number of Nazi ghettos or camps in Europe:
42,500

First camp to be liberated:
Majdanek, Poland, July 23, 1944

U.S. troops examine victims

CHAPTER 5

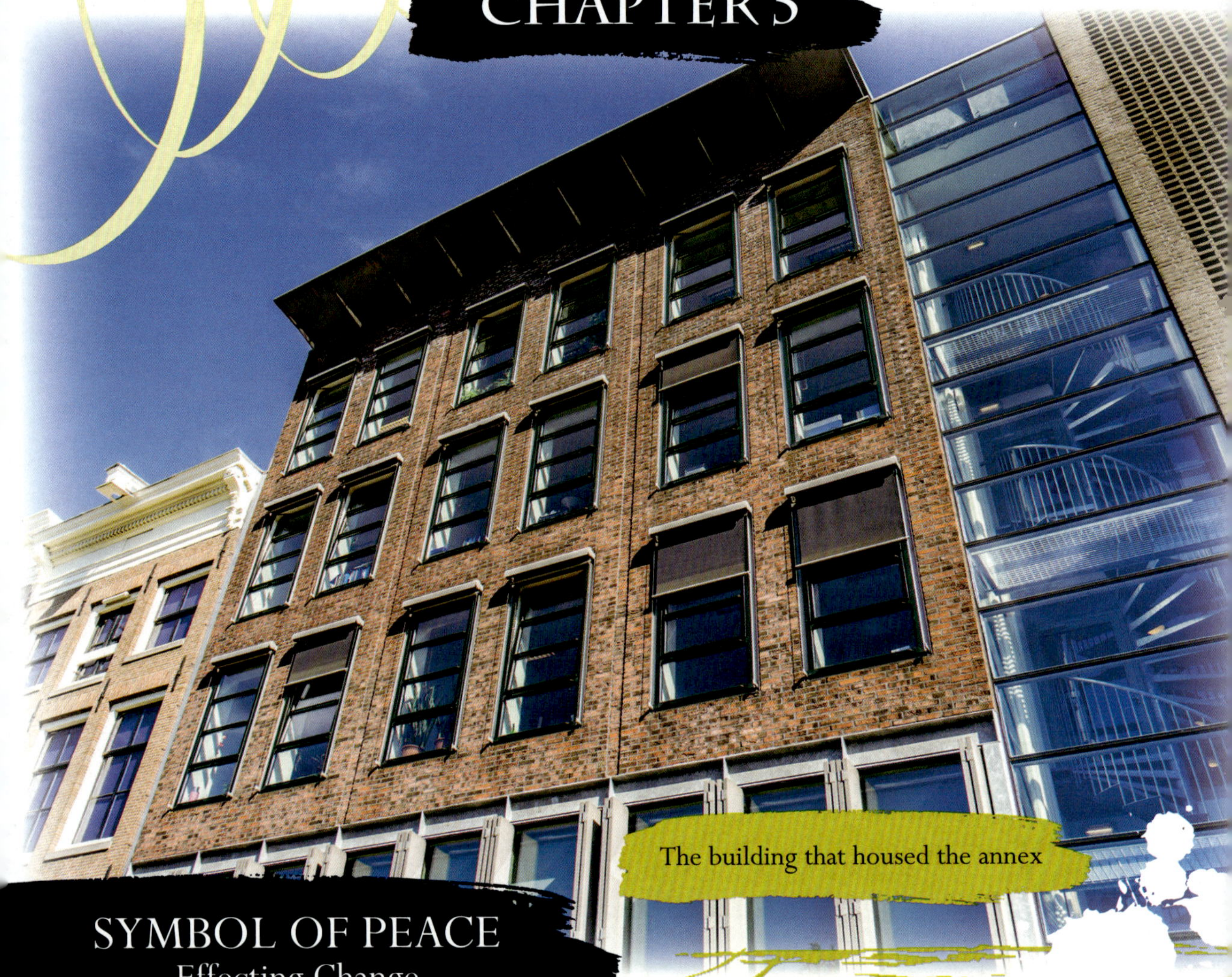

The building that housed the annex

SYMBOL OF PEACE
Effecting Change

The last stages of Anne's life:

Last diary entry: August 1, 1944

Family discovered: August 4, 1944

Anne deported from Holland: September 3, 1944

Arrived at Auschwitz: September 6, 1944

Transported to Bergen-Belsen: November 1, 1944

Died of typhus: Late February/ Early March 1945

Bergen-Belsen liberated: April 12, 1945

Anne writes that she somehow FEELS that things will CHANGE and IMPROVE, and that the CRUELTY of the Nazis will STOP. Anne believes that the world will return to PEACE again. She says that until that happens she will HOLD ON to her dreams and HOPES and that maybe one day they WILL come true.

CAPTURED

On August 4, 1944, what everyone in the annex had dreaded most came true. They heard men in the office downstairs demanding to know where the Jews were hiding. The next thing they knew, armed Nazi police stormed upstairs. Somebody had given them away.

The police rounded up everyone and told them to pack up their valuables. One picked up the briefcase in which Anne's diary, notebooks, and other papers were stored. The books fell to the floor, but no one bothered to pick them up. When an officer asked Otto how long the families had been hiding, he did not believe they had been there for nearly two years. To show he was not lying, Otto pointed to the wall where he had measured Anne's growing height since they arrived in the annex.

Somebody had given them away.

After Anne and the others had been taken away, Miep crept into the annex. She knew the Nazis would come back to clear everything out. Miep wanted to gather up Anne's papers, because she knew Anne had kept her diary all the time she was in hiding. Miep took everything she could find, including the family's photograph albums, and locked them in a drawer in her office. She wanted to return them to the Franks if they ever returned.

After their capture, the residents of the annex were arrested. They were sent to a transit camp in northern Holland. They were then deported to concentration camps in Poland.

Words that changed the world

In 1942, Anne writes that German military vehicles are cruising along the streets. The Nazis are knocking on every door and asking if any Jews live there. If they find Jews, the Germans take them away. The Germans even offer money to the Dutch people to give information about Jews. Anne says it is like the slave hunts of the past. She describes seeing long lines of Jewish people walking along the street, pushed on by the Nazi soldiers and beaten by them until they nearly drop to the ground.

These movie actors in Amsterdam are recreating the return of Jews after the war.

Exploring the text

Anne vividly describes what life was like for Amsterdam's Jews who were not in hiding. The forced registration of all the city's Jews made it easy for the Gestapo (the Nazi secret police) to locate Jewish families. As the war continued, it became harder for Jewish families to flee. The experience of the Franks and the van Pels was not unique. In all, around 28,000 Jews in Holland were forced into hiding during World War II.

HISTORY'S STORY

It remains a mystery who betrayed the Frank family to the Gestapo. It was none of the helpers from the office, and no one ever confessed. Yet it is clear that somebody did tell the Germans. The officers who raided the annex knew someone was hiding there. Were the families betrayed for money or for some other reason?

REDISCOVERY OF THE DIARY

The eight residents of the annex were sent to different concentration camps in Poland. Over the next year, all of them except Otto Frank died. He was liberated from Auschwitz concentration camp when Soviet troops arrived there on January 27, 1945.

Otto eventually returned to Amsterdam after the defeat of Germany and the death of Adolf Hitler. He arrived back in the city on June 3, 1945. He still had no idea about what had happened to his wife or daughters. The last time he had seen them was when they were separated on their arrival at Auschwitz. Otto spent the first six months back in Amsterdam looking for his family and the others. He placed advertisements in newspapers asking if anyone had any information about his daughters. By the end of the year, he knew that he was the only one of his family who had survived.

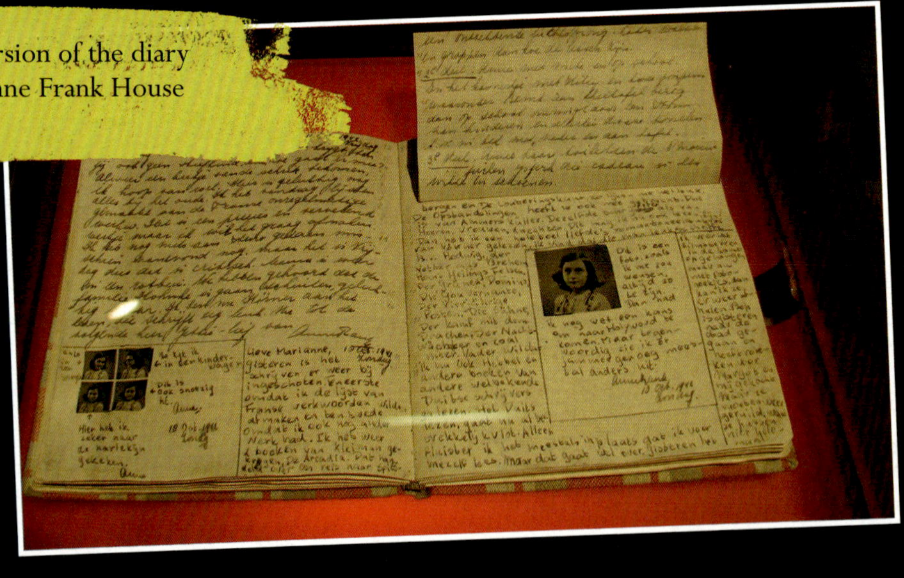

The original version of the diary is kept at the Anne Frank House in Amsterdam.

When Otto returned to Amsterdam, Miep Gies found him much thinner than when he had been in hiding. Miep still had Anne's diary. Although Anne had given most people false names, she had used the real names of the family's helpers. If the Nazis had read the diary, these helpers would have been put to death.

A daughter revealed

Otto read his daughter's diary. He could not believe Anne had felt all the different emotions she had written down. Otto later said that reading the diary had overwhelmed him—it had showed him a completely different side to Anne. He decided to translate the diary from Dutch into German for his immediate family so that they could learn about what happened in the annex. As he copied Anne's words, he realized that his daughter had been a very talented writer.

This photograph shows Miep Gies (left) with her husband (center) and Otto Frank (right) in 1961.

HISTORY'S STORY

Otto did not initially intend to publish Anne's diary, mainly because of how Anne wrote about her family a lot of the time. The more he read it, however, the more he realized the diary was a unique historical document and that his daughter had been a talented writer. Given her ambition to be published, he decided to get the diary into print.

SYMBOL OF INNOCENCE

While the family was in hiding, Anne heard a radio broadcast from the headquarters of the exiled Dutch government in London, England. On March 29, 1944, the education minister asked the Dutch people to save any letters and diaries written during the occupation. He thought they would be an important record of a key part of Dutch history. Anne started rewriting her diary so that it could be used as a record of their time in hiding. She had not finished this version before the Gestapo raid.

This mural of Anne Frank was painted on the side of a house in Berlin in 2014.

As Otto translated the two versions of Anne's diary into a single German version, he realized that it was an important historical document. It described frankly what life had been like for a teenager and her family persecuted by the Nazis. Still, however, he was reluctant to let anybody outside the family read the diary because Anne was so brutally honest. It was not a flattering portrait of the Franks.

After Otto's family read the diary, they convinced him to share it with a wider audience. Two Dutch historians tried to get the diary published in 1946. One of them wrote an article for a newspaper. He claimed that Anne's diary revealed the real horrors of the Nazis much more clearly than the Nuremberg trials, which were then being held to try Nazi leaders as war criminals.

Into print

On June 25, 1947, the diary was published as *Het Achterhuis* (*The Secret Annex*). It sold out. However, it was not until 1952 that an English version was published after an editor at Doubleday, a publishing house in New York City, found it on a pile of rejected manuscripts. The introduction to the U.S. edition was written by the former First Lady, Eleanor Roosevelt. She called the book "one of the wisest and most moving commentaries on war and its impact on human beings that I have ever read."

The book became a best seller around the world. As its popularity grew, the title was changed to *Anne Frank: The Diary of a Young Girl*. Anne became a symbol of the wasted innocence destroyed not just by the Holocaust but by warfare in general. To date, the diary has been translated into more than 70 languages.

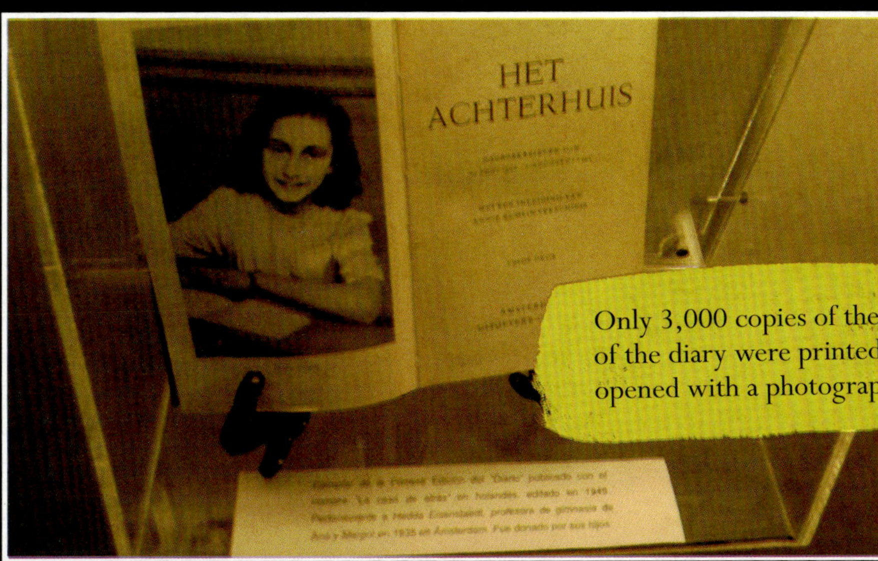

Only 3,000 copies of the first edition of the diary were printed. The book opened with a photograph of Anne.

FACTS AND FIGURES ABOUT *THE DIARY OF A YOUNG GIRL*

It was translated into more than 70 languages.

To date, more than 30 million copies have been sold.

In the United States, 10 publishers initially turned down the manuscript.

The first U.S. print run was just 5,000 copies.

A photograph of Anne on a stamp from the Netherlands

Otto Frank shows the book to a group of Japanese visitors to the Anne Frank House.

After a favorable review in the *New York Times*, a second edition of 15,000 copies was printed. Another edition of 45,000 copies appeared a few days later.

It was published in West Germany in 1950, just five years after the end of the war.

This entry from the diary comes from September 28, 1942.

CHAPTER 6

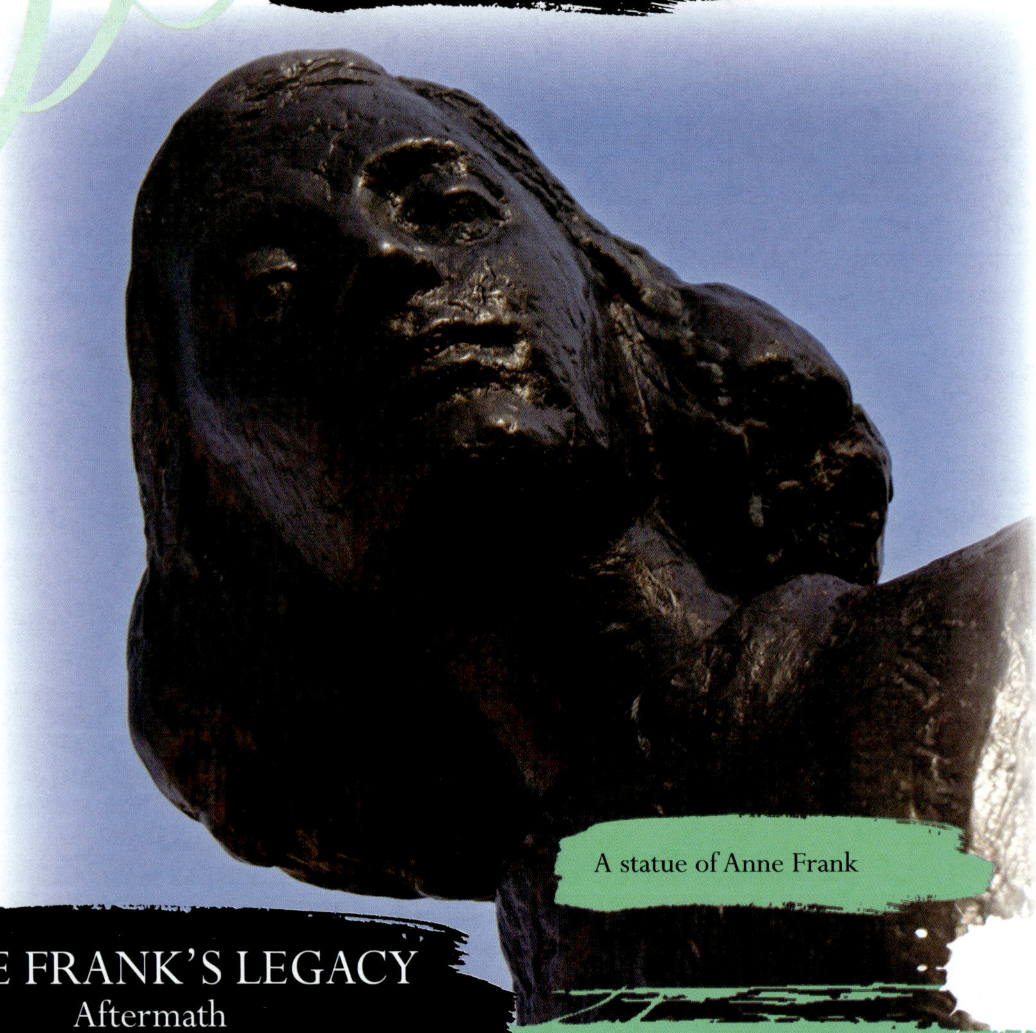

A statue of Anne Frank

ANNE FRANK'S LEGACY
Aftermath

Anne's lasting legacy:

More than 30 million copies of *Anne Frank: The Diary of a Young Girl* sold

Translated into more than 70 languages

Anne Frank House—more than 1.2 million visitors a year

Anne Frank Foundation—promoting peace

Humanitarian organizations devoted to her legacy

Educational programs promoting tolerance and understanding

Anne's LEGACY is undeniable. The WRITINGS of this young teenage girl have had an ENORMOUS IMPACT on the world. Today, Anne's diary is used to TEACH children around the WORLD about the HOLOCAUST and to warn against PREJUDICE and HATRED of people just because of their RACE or BELIEFS.

KEEPING ANNE'S SPIRIT ALIVE

Otto Frank's initial ambitions when he returned to Amsterdam from Auschwitz were to reunite his family. Soon, he realized that nobody else was coming back. It was a terrible time, and he struggled to cope with his loss. He had no choice but to start a new life.

Soon, he realized that nobody else was coming back.

This is a memorial to Anne in Frankfurt, which was her birthplace in Germany.

Otto studied the notebooks and photographs Miep had saved. As he read Anne's diary, he saw a new side to his daughter. There were parts of his daughter's account of the problems of being a teenager that shocked him. But he was also moved by her bravery and optimism. Despite his own reluctance, his family persuaded him to make Anne's dream of being a writer come true.

As soon as the book was published in Holland in 1947, it was clear that the diary had a remarkable appeal to readers. Most of its early readers had lived through the war themselves, but the diary has continued to fascinate people born long after the conflict. As well as becoming a best seller, the diary has been turned into movies, TV shows, and stage plays. A Broadway play opened in 1955 and was the basis of the 1959 movie *The Diary of Anne Frank*, which won three Oscars.

Words that changed the world

In 1944, Anne writes that for a long time she has hoped to one day become a journalist and then a famous writer. She says that only time will tell if her crazy dreams come true! She says that one day she would like to publish a book called The Secret Annex. *Anne notes that her diary will be used as the starting point for the book.*

Otto Frank was a very private man, but he overcame his own reservations about publishing Anne's diary.

Exploring the text

Anne mentions more than once in her diary her desire to become a writer when the war is over and she returns to normal life. She has outgrown her earlier ambition to be a movie star. Her observation that she has had no lack of topics can be seen as being a little ironic, given that she had been confined to the annex for over a year. It is clear that she has begun to think for the first time about the possibility that her words will one day be read by other people. She clearly hopes that the diary will serve as a record of what life had been like for her in hiding.

HISTORY'S STORY

Anne was clear about her ambitions for the future. What would she think about the fact that her diary is one of the most famous diaries ever published? Or that she is one of the best-selling writers of all time?

ANNE AND AMSTERDAM

Before the Frank family was forced into hiding in 1942, Anne loved living in Amsterdam. She and her many friends skated on the city's frozen canals in the winter and the beach was not too far away. She liked the Dutch and decided that she would become a Dutch citizen once the war was over. She was happy to learn to speak and write Dutch. She even wrote her diary in Dutch. In addition, the Dutch had their own royal family—and Anne loved royalty!

The secret annex was above Otto's office at the headquarters of Opekta, a fruit-extract business. Otto chose it as a hiding place because it was concealed from view by surrounding buildings. After the war, he decided to turn the annex into a museum. Work started in 1957 to restore the building, which by then had become very run down. Otto said that he believed that, as well as being a museum, the annex should act as somewhere that people could go to to think about the Holocaust and reflect on it. The museum finally opened in 1960. At first it was free to visit, but since 1971 an entrance fee has been charged.

What happened to Anne and Margot's bodies is unknown. This is a symbolic gravestone at Bergen-Belsen.

A popular destination

Today, the Anne Frank House is one of the most popular tourist attractions in Amsterdam. The annex has been restored to how it was during the war. The furniture has been removed, but Anne's torn-out magazine pictures of her favorite movie stars are preserved on the wall of her bedroom. To reach the annex, visitors climb up to the Opekta offices, which have also been restored to their wartime appearance. Then visitors reach the landing and the bookcase that conceals the hidden annex. Climbing up the narrow stairs into the tiny rooms where the eight residents lived for more than two years, the biggest impression visitors get is how cramped a space it is. After leaving the annex, visitors enter an exhibition space where they can learn more about what they have seen.

More reminders

There are more reminders of Anne and her family around Amsterdam. In 2005, a man named Jimmink owned the bookstore where Otto bought Anne's red-and-white checked diary for her 13th birthday. Jimmink had a small bronze statue of Anne erected close to Merwedeplein, where the Franks lived from 1933 until they went into hiding. Anne carries two heavy bags. Another bronze statue of Anne is located close to the museum by the church whose bells Anne could hear from the annex. Without doubt, Anne is the most famous resident ever to have lived in Amsterdam.

This statue of Anne stands close to the Franks' home before they went into hiding.

THE ANNE FRANK FOUNDATION

Anne's legacy goes beyond her diary and the Anne Frank House. Many different foundations across the world bear her name. In 1957, after Otto decided that the annex must be saved, the Anne Frank Foundation was set up in the Netherlands to ensure the preservation of the old house, which was threatened with demolition. Today, the foundation's work goes much further. It is involved in education and in monitoring anti-Semitism and racism. Many people fear such extreme ideas are on the increase across Europe once again.

Tourists stand in line for their chance to enter the Anne Frank House beside a canal in Amsterdam.

Otto also set up the Anne Frank Fonds (Foundation) in 1963. It is a nonprofit organization that controls all of Anne's writings and material belonging to the Frank family, including photographs. The millions of dollars it has generated have helped thousands of young people.

Otto Frank shows visitors the stove the families used for cooking in the annex.

A powerful symbol

Otto wanted the foundation to help improve understanding between societies and religions and to improve relations between people of different nations. Its message is tolerance and understanding. Today, Anne Frank stands as a symbol in the battle against racism, anti-Semitism, and fascism. The message of her diary is that people should oppose racism and fascism and protect the rights of women and children. Anne wanted a fairer and more just society, which is what the foundations named for her promote across the world.

HISTORY'S STORY

Otto Frank slowly rebuilt his life after the war. In 1953, he moved to Switzerland to be near his sister and her family. That same year, he remarried. His second wife, Elfriede Markovits Geiringer, had survived the concentration camps. Otto died on August 19, 1980, at age 91. Until his death, he devoted his life to spreading Anne's hopeful message of peace and reconciliation.

THE DIARY ON SCREEN

Movies

1959: *The Diary of Anne Frank* (winner of three Oscars) U.S.

1995: *Anne Frank Remembered* U.S./U.K./NETHERLANDS

1995: *Anne no Nikki* (anime) JAPAN

1999: *Le Journal d'Anne Frank* (animated) FRANCE

2016: *Das Tagebuch der Anne Frank* GERMANY

Memorials to the Frank family in Amsterdam

TV Series

1958: *Das Tagebuch der Anne Frank* EAST GERMANY

1962: *Het Dagboek van Anne Frank* NETHERLANDS

1967: *The Diary of Anne Frank* U.S.

1980: *The Diary of Anne Frank* U.S.

1987: *The Diary of Anne Frank* U.K.

1988: *The Attic: The Hiding of Anne Frank* U.S.

1988: *The Last Seven Months of Anne Frank* NETHERLANDS

2001: *The Short Life of Anne Frank* NETHERLANDS

2009: *The Diary of Anne Frank* U.K.

2009: *Mi Ricordo Anna Frank* ITALY

2015: *Meine Tochter Anne Frank* GERMANY

2015: *No Asylum: The Untold Chapter in Anne Frank's Story* U.S.

The actress Ellie Kendrick playing Anne Frank

A German stamp featuring Anne Frank

GLOSSARY

ambition a desire to achieve something
annex a building or apartment added to another building to provide extra space
anti-Semitism a hatred of Jewish people
chancellor the head of government in Germany
concentration camps places where large numbers of people are held captive in a small space with poor facilities
confidant someone with whom one shares personal secrets
confinement being limited to a small space
confiscate take someone's property
deported removed a foreigner from a country
economic related to money and business
emigrate to leave one country to move to another
exile the state of being banned from one's own native country
extermination the killing of a whole group of people
fascism a political approach that treats the individual as less important than their country
fluently speaking a language easily
forced labor a system in which people are made to work for nothing, often by harsh punishments
foundation an organization that provides money to support a particular cause
Gestapo the secret police of Nazi Germany
ghettos run-down parts of cities inhabited by only one minority group
Hanukkah a Jewish festival marked by lighting a series of candles
Holocaust the name for the mass murder of the Jews and other people during World War II
inferior less important than
ironic interesting or funny, usually because something is different from what is expected
Kristallnacht German for "the night of broken glass," describing the night of November 9/10, 1938, when Nazis attacked Jewish businesses and smashed their windows
labor camp a place where people are kept captive and forced to work
liberated released from captivity
manuscripts books or documents written by hand
material related to physical things
memorial a monument to remind people of someone or something
menorah a holder with seven or nine candles that is used in Jewish worship
military laws laws that are imposed and enforced by the army rather than by civilian courts
mortality the fact that everyone will inevitably die
Nazis people who follow the beliefs of the Nazi Party, which promoted nationalism and racism and a military sense of order and discipline
occupation the act of a country using its military forces to control another country
occupied invaded and took over another country
persecution the ill treatment of a group of people because of their race, religion, or other qualities
registration the recording of names and other information on an official list
relocate to move to a new location
sacrifice giving up something valuable in the hopes of benefiting in other ways
smuggled illegally moved something to a destination
status position or importance in society
strategic related to the long-term goals of a military campaign
swastika a Nazi symbol of a cross with each of its four arms broken at right angles
synagogues Jewish places of worship
tolerance acceptance of other people and their beliefs
transit camp a place where prisoners are held temporarily during a journey
typhus an infectious disease that is often fatal
volunteers people who willingly do something for no financial reward
warehouse a large building for storing raw materials and goods

FOR MORE INFORMATION

BOOKS

Bell, Samantha. *Children in the Holocaust*. Lake Elmo, MN: Focus Readers, 2019.

Burling, Alexis. *Anne Frank: Holocaust Diarist*. Minneapolis, MN: Essential Library, 2017.

Cooke, Tim. *Anne Frank*. New York, NY: Gareth Stevens Publishing, 2019.

Radomski, Kassandra. *Anne Frank: Get to Know the Girl Beyond Her Diary*. North Mankato, MN: Capstone Press, 2019.

WEBSITES

Anne Frank—www.bbc.co.uk/annefrank/timeline.shtml
This page includes a timeline of the major events of Anne's life.

Anne Frank House—www.annefrank.org/en
Read all about the Anne Frank House in Amsterdam.

Biography: Anne Frank—
www.ducksters.com/biography/women_leaders/anne_frank.php
Learn more about Anne Frank's life here.

Publisher's note to educators and parents: Our editors have carefully reviewed these websites to ensure that they are suitable for students. Many websites change frequently, however, and we cannot guarantee that a site's future contents will continue to meet our high standards of quality and educational value. Be advised that students should be closely supervised whenever they access the Internet.

INDEX